An Educator's Guide to
Field-based Classroom Observation

HOUGHTON MIFFLIN **GUIDE** **SERIES**

An Educator's Guide to
Field-based Classroom Observation

Gary D. Borich
The University of Texas at Austin

James M. Cooper, Series Editor
University of Virginia

HOUGHTON MIFFLIN COMPANY   BOSTON   NEW YORK

Senior Sponsoring Editor: Sue Pulvermacher-Alt
Senior Development Editor: Lisa Mafrici
Editorial Associate: Sara Hauschildt
Editorial Assistant: Trinity Peacock-Broyles
Senior Manufacturing Manager: Florence Cadran
Marketing Manager: Jane Potter

Printed in the U.S.A.

ISBN: 0-618-41274-3

23456789-QUE-12 11 10 09 08

CONTENTS

PREFACE

Houghton Mifflin Company publishes outstanding education textbooks in the areas of foundations of education, introduction to education, educational psychology special education, and early childhood education. These textbooks introduce students to many concepts, policies, and research that undergird educational practice. However, as is the case for virtually all introductory texts, many topics are introduced but not covered in great depth. The Houghton Mifflin Teacher Education Guide Series is designed to provide more in-depth coverage of selected educational topics studied in the teacher education curriculum.

At the present time, there are seven guides in the series:

- Classroom Management
- Field-based Classroom Observation
- Diversity in the Classroom
- Classroom Assessment
- Inclusion
- Technology Tools
- School-based Intervention Programs

The topics for these guides were selected because they are addressed in virtually all teacher education programs, and contain vital information for beginning teachers if they are to be successful in the classroom. Instructors may use the guides either for required or enrichment reading.

Each of these guides provides pre-service teachers with greater in-depth knowledge, application suggestions, and additional resources on its particular topic. All the guides share a common format that includes an introduction to the topic, knowledge that the prospective teacher should possess about the topic, examples of and suggestions for how the knowledge can be applied, and resources for further exploration. Each guide also contains 10-15 questions designed to help the prospective teacher reflect on the concepts and ideas introduced in the guide, as well as a glossary of key terms.

Most teacher education programs now provide many opportunities for prospective teachers to observe in school classrooms and to partake in instructional activities. Integrating pedagogical training with experiences in schools allows teacher education students to merge theory with practice. In this guide, Gary Borich identifies key concepts and tools for helping teacher education students to focus their classroom observations so as to understand better the busy and complex interactions occurring in school classrooms. One researcher found that as many as 1000 interactions occur daily in elementary classrooms! Seeing and understanding what is happening in classrooms is not easy and requires considerable training and practice. Borich provides a number of different research-based lenses for viewing classroom behavior, and practice exercises to develop interpretative skill to make sense of the data collected. As prospective teachers take these tools into classrooms to collect and interpret information on classroom behavior, they will gain deeper understanding of the teaching and learning that occurs there.

The Educator's Guide to

eld-based Classroom
bservation

PART I: INTRODUCTION*

Playing in the park, 3-year-old Jake looks up to see his mother approaching. He runs down the sidewalk to greet her. In his haste, he trips on an uneven stone and lands, unceremoniously, at his mother's feet.

For a moment, Jake looks stunned—about to cry. His mother wonders if he is hurt as he glances up at her face with a questioning look.

Laughing, Jake's mother scoops him into her arms. "Hi, honey!" she chuckles. "What fun to have you so excited to see me!"

The imminent clouds on Jake's face clear, and the toddler smiles.

How often have you observed a similar event—noting that split second when a child seems to decide how to respond to a given situation? Like Jake, each of us experiences many interactions with the world every day. As we try to make sense of these events, we create a personal framework or set of expectations about the nature of the world and our appropriate responses to events within it. This set of expectations influences what we see in a particular setting, as well as what we choose to ignore.

Many psychologists believe that professionals create frames for understanding within their chosen fields, just as individuals construct a frame for interpreting the events of daily life. Experts know what to look for and rapidly learn from what they see, and thereby rise to the top of their profession long before others who do not have a structure for sorting out the least relevant from the most relevant details. Sternberg (1995) believes that intelligent behavior may be marked more by the structure or frame one brings to a problem or task than by what one knows about the problem or task beforehand. Thus, developing a **professional frame** from which to evaluate and act objectively on events is a critical skill for becoming an expert.

---

* For further content on the field-based observation techniques in this booklet, see Borich, G. (2003). *Observation Skills for Effective Teaching,* (4th ed.). Upper Saddle River, NJ: Merrill/Prentice-Hall. The author thanks Debra Bayles Martin for contributions that appear in this booklet.

From observing the actions and interactions of professionals, less experienced individuals gain a sense of what is valued in a particular discipline and how professionals working in that field typically respond to events. But, while observation seems as simple and commonplace as dressing, eating, or driving a car, it is important to remember that, like Jake, each of us interprets the world and responds to it according to our personal frame. Without some outside direction, it is possible that our classroom observations may serve to validate much of what we already "expect" to see—allowing us to overemphasize some things and overlook others. As a result, observations need to be focused if they are to be helpful in our professional life.

The field-based observation techniques for the training of teachers come from more than twenty-five years of research on effective teaching and from national standards for the teaching profession representing how students and teachers best learn. For decades, teaching reflected a direct instruction model, where teachers were expected to present or "transmit" knowledge to students—who were expected to receive, store, and return information upon request. Many researchers and educators have challenged this view, suggesting that learners do not simply "receive" knowledge; rather, they actively construct knowledge through interacting with the social, cultural, and linguistic context in which an experience occurs (Richardson, 1997). Effective teachers function as able facilitators, coaches, and guides for students' knowledge-building processes.

Reflecting this more interactive view of teaching, the **National Board for Professional Teaching Standards (NBPTS)** was formed in 1987 with three major goals:

1. To establish high and rigorous standards for what accomplished teachers should know and be able to do;

2. To develop and operate a national, voluntary system to assess and certify teachers who meet these standards;

3. To advance related education reforms for the purpose of improving student learning in American schools.

During that same year, the **Interstate New Teacher Assessment and Support Consortium (INTASC)** was formed to create "board-compatible" standards that could be reviewed by professional organizations and state agencies as a basis for licensing beginning teachers. The INTASC standards (Miller, 1992) are written as 10 principles, which are then further explained in terms of teacher knowledge, dispositions, and performance. In other words, they describe what a beginning teacher should know and be able to do. Listed below are these 10 principles, which were intended in part to be acquired through field-based observation.

Principle 1:

The teacher understands the central concepts, tools of inquiry, and structures of the discipline(s) he or she teaches and can create learning experiences that make these aspects of subject matter meaningful for students.

Principle 2:

The teacher understands how children learn and develop, and can provide learning opportunities that support their intellectual, social and personal development.

Principle 3:

The teacher understands how students differ in their approaches to learning and creates instructional opportunities that are adapted to diverse learners.

Principle 4:

The teacher understands and uses a variety of instructional strategies to encourage students' development of critical thinking, problem solving, and performance skills.

Principle 5:

The teacher uses an understanding of individual and group motivation and behavior to create a learning environment that encourages positive social interaction, active engagement in learning, and self-motivation.

Principle 6:

The teacher uses knowledge of effective verbal, nonverbal, and media communication techniques to foster active inquiry, collaboration, and supportive interaction in the classroom.

Principle 7:

The teacher plans instruction based upon knowledge of subject matter, students, the community, and curriculum goals.

Principle 8:

The teacher understands and uses formal and informal assessment strategies to evaluate and ensure the continuous intellectual, social and physical development of the learner.

Principle 9:

The teacher is a reflective practitioner who continually evaluates the effects of his/her choices and actions on others (students, parents, and other professionals in the learning community) and who actively seeks out opportunities to grow professionally.

Principle 10:

The teacher fosters relationships with school colleagues, parents, and agencies in the larger community to support students' learning and well-being.

Much of classroom observation focuses on ways you can observe other teachers to learn about the teaching profession. The information you gain from these observations will help you expand your professional framework to include insights about teaching which follow the INTASC and NBPTS standards. But, classroom observation also addresses ways to apply observation techniques and insights to your own teaching. Thus, while you are observing others to learn about their approaches to teaching, you will also be learning to observe yourself— and to be observed by others. These observations can provide important insights about your growth and development as a teacher.

PART II: KNOWLEDGE

GOALS FOR FOCUSED OBSERVATIONS

The ability to consciously consider your personal growth is called *reflection*. There are many goals you will want to work toward in order to reflect on your own behavior. But some of the most important for focused observations are to achieve empathy, establish cooperative relationships, become realistic, establish direction, attain confidence, express enthusiasm, become flexible, and become self-reliant. As you observe professionals working to achieve each of these goals, you will want to reflect on your own development—and then set some goals for yourself. Because a cycle of observation, reflection, and goal setting is so important to becoming a productive and successful professional, let's consider these eight goals for focused observation in more detail.

Goal 1: To Achieve Empathy

Effective teachers exhibit *empathy*—a willingness to see events from different points of view and to appreciate others' interpretations or reasons for acting the way they do. An empathic approach can help you to understand student behavior from the student's point of view—which often provides insights for effective ways of dealing with problems or challenges. Your ability to empathize during classroom observations will serve you well both as an observer and as a teacher. For example, when you observe a teacher implementing an unusual classroom rule, you may be tempted to pass judgment on the teacher's effectiveness or on the rule's appropriateness—from your point of view. While your own experiences are an important source of information in evaluating what you observe, you will also benefit from trying to understand events from the teacher's vantage point. You may ask yourself, "Is what I am seeing working within the context of this classroom? Why or why not?" As you consider these questions, you may discover that a seemingly ineffective strategy in one context may be effective in another. As a result, your observations will extend beyond your personal and textbook knowledge of teaching to include an awareness of the variety of social and learning contexts that can influence a teacher's decisions. Enhancing your ability to empathize will help you approach your own teaching with more flexibility—and with the instructional alternatives you need to be an effective teacher.

Goal 2: To Establish Cooperative Relationships

Early on, effective teachers identify people who can help them in their teaching. They understand that, in the hectic and stressful environment of the classroom, people need other people to offer ideas, support, and collegiality. As you become involved in student teaching, and later in your beginning years of teaching, you will find a need to develop cooperative relationships with your colleagues. Experienced teachers have a wealth of information about students, curriculum, textbooks, and media with which you will be working. As you observe in different classrooms, you can and should take the opportunity to discover how professionals create and maintain cooperative relationships and how you can become an active participant in these relationships. These experienced teachers can answer many questions you will have now—and later.

Goal 3: To Become Realistic

Most beginning teachers understandably have an idealistic view of schools and teaching. While idealism motivates us to renew and extend our efforts, it also creates pitfalls when we are unreasonable in our expectations of students or ourselves. For example, beginning teachers who believe that schools *should be* a certain way may spend a great deal of time and effort trying to change a particular setting—failing to see and accept the strengths of the context they are working with. From your classroom observations, you will learn that schools and classrooms vary widely—and that each context offers both advantages and challenges. As you observe and reflect upon different classrooms, you will become more realistic in evaluating both what is desirable and what is possible in different classrooms.

Goal 4: To Establish Direction

Another purpose of classroom observation is to establish the professional goals toward which you will want to work during your student teaching and first years of teaching. By observing others, you will identify characteristics and practices you will want to emulate in your own teaching. Recording these characteristics and practices during observation can form the basis of short- and long-term goals of self-improvement. One of the advantages of focused observation is the opportunity to identify particular patterns and sequences of teacher behavior and to evaluate their effectiveness in a variety of settings. Over time, you should be able to identify teaching strategies specific to particular purposes and contexts that you value and to integrate them into your own teaching.

Goal 5: To Attain Confidence

Most of us in the course of learning to become teachers make judgments about what we believe is effective teaching. In the course of teaching, we then make decisions that follow from these judgments. Many of these decisions about what and how to teach represent gut feelings, the exact source of which may not be known to us. Some writers refer to this way of knowing as *tacit or practical knowledge* (Canning, 1991). Tacit knowledge represents what we know by experience, but rarely, if ever, articulate. Just as in the example with Jake, each of us compiles vast amounts of tacit knowledge through everyday experiences. This knowledge often guides our actions as effectively as does the knowledge we gain from formal instruction. Our tacit knowledge is put to use by acting, sometimes unconsciously, on thoughts and feelings acquired from day-to-day experiences. Tacitly acquired knowledge often helps us distinguish what is right from wrong, appropriate from inappropriate, and effective from ineffective. Through observation, beginning teachers learn to test their judgments and to trust their instincts.

Goal 6: To Express Enthusiasm

Effective teachers demonstrate an enthusiasm for the subject matter they teach, and for the teaching profession. The ability to express enthusiasm stems from a belief that what we do matters. Having an image of a future self who is growing provides us with the courage to work hard and attain the goals we select. You can enhance your personal enthusiasm and learn to calm your fears by seeing others attain goals, perform activities, and produce results that you would like to accomplish. As you observe successful teachers, you will find yourself saying, "I want to be like that." From this, you will set goals such as, "I want to *try* that." As you try various techniques, you then discover that you *can* accomplish particular goals, and your enthusiasm for teaching grows. Focused observation of successful and enthusiastic teachers can help you dare to express the enthusiasm within you.

Goal 7: To Become Flexible

A part of setting and achieving any goal is being willing to take risks. Effective teachers most often achieve their goals in the context of trial and error. This means that to develop as a professional, you must try new things and risk occasional failure. We seldom succeed in attaining a goal, performing an activity, or achieving the desired results the first time we try something. The key to our improvement is to persevere long enough for success to occur. Since some struggle is inevitable in becoming an effective teacher, it is important to develop a flexible attitude. For example, you may practice a behavior exactly as you observed it in a particular classroom—and not achieve the desired results. This is the time to consider various aspects of the behavior that could be adapted or altered in some way. The fact that you have observed teachers in many different settings will likely suggest variations you can try to improve your strategy. In other words, as you observe teachers implementing a strategy in different ways, you, too, can gain the ability to see and act more flexibly in your own teaching.

Goal 8: To Become Self-reliant

Perhaps the most important goal of focused classroom observation is becoming self-reliant. As you observe across many educational contexts, you will be building a professional frame from which to interpret events and make decisions. The greater the detail and scope of your observations, the greater your sense of personal confidence, enthusiasm, and flexibility will be in achieving your goals. Focused observation in classrooms will reveal that teaching is a complex profession for which no amount of formal training can provide all the preparation needed. It will also underscore the fact that effective teachers exist because of the challenges of teaching and that, with careful reflection and effort you can be one of them.

PROFESSIONAL GOALS FOR IMPROVEMENT

As you prepare to observe in classrooms, it is important to consider what sort of "lens" you will observe through. All of us develop our own views of the world or ways of looking at life. Our view is influenced throughout our lives by the experiences we have, the emotions we feel, and the way we choose to interpret them. What are the characteristics of your world view? How might they affect the way you "see" particular teachers or classrooms? Let's try a little experiment to find out. Read the sentences below (from a study by Sanford & Garrod, 1981, p. 114) and create a mental picture from the words.

John was on his way to school.

What picture formed in your mind as you read the sentence? How old is John? What does he look like? What time of day is it? What is the weather like? Remember what you pictured and read on.

He was terribly worried about the math lesson.

Now what is the picture you see? Has it changed? Does being worried about a math lesson "fit" the picture you have already developed in your mind about what John is like? Keep reading.

He thought he might not be able to control the class again today.

Has anything in your mental picture changed? What? Why? Now keep reading.

It was not a normal part of a janitor's duties.

What do you see now in your mental picture? How old is John? What does he look like? Were you surprised at the information in the last sentence? Why?

Just as you formed mental images and expectations while reading about John, you have probably formed a number of mental images and expectations about schools and classrooms. To explore a few of these images, take a minute and make a list with the following headings:

The perfect classroom	The perfect teacher	The perfect lesson
(how it looks, smells, feels, etc.)	(his or her classroom management, instructional methods and presentation style, etc.)	(subject, duration, type of activities, etc.)

Source: From Borich, G. (2003). *Observation Skills for Effective Teaching,* 4th edition. Upper Saddle River, NJ: Merrill/Prentice Hall. This and the following graphic reprinted with permission.

Now, take a minute to create a second list with these headings.

A terrible classroom	A terrible teacher	A terrible lesson
(how it looks, smells, feels, etc.)	(his or her classroom management, instructional methods and presentation style, etc.)	(subject, duration, type of activities, etc.)

What do you notice about the two lists you have created? Can you think of any specific experiences that may have influenced each of your lists?

WHAT REAL CLASSROOMS ARE LIKE

As you make formal and informal observations on your way to becoming a teacher, it is important to realize that you are about to enter a complex and demanding profession—a profession that requires not only intelligence, physical stamina, and motivation, but also an acute sense of sight and sound. Your ability to perceive what is happening in a classroom will be critical to your success as a teacher. Because the teaching profession is complex, it is important for you to consider how your preconceived ideas about teaching and students may influence what you see and hear—and how you interpret that information. No doubt you have already formed, from your years as a student, a set of beliefs about good and poor teaching, teachers, students, and lessons. While these opinions and beliefs comprise an important part of your view of education, they can also act as "blinders," and even limit your teaching goals for particular students or settings (Walqui, 2000). In order to look beyond personal experience to obtain a more complete view of classrooms, let's consider four characteristics of classrooms that will affect what you see: *rapidity, immediacy, interruption,* and *social dynamics.*

Rapidity

One of the first things you will notice from observing in classrooms is that events move rapidly. In fact, some authors have estimated that there are up to one thousand teacher-student interchanges in most classrooms in a single day. These interchanges include asking questions, soliciting information, clarifying answers, probing for details, reciting facts, and responding to student requests. In other words, events do not move slowly in classrooms; they are constantly changing at a rapid rate from teacher question to student response, and from student question back to teacher response—creating a momentum of classroom activity that puts the teacher on the front lines practically every minute of the day. The teacher's ability to move the class along at a brisk pace, keep transitions between major instructional events short and orderly, and establish milestones toward which all students work contributes momentum and a sense of accomplishment to the classroom. Being able to see how rapidly changing events in a classroom can be used to establish momentum is an important observation skill.

Immediacy

Closely related to the rapidity of life in classrooms is the immediacy of the interactions that occur within them. Immediacy pertains to the need to respond quickly to rapidly occurring events. For example, teachers often do not have time to think about how they will respond to a student question, but rather must have an answer—some answer—ready for almost any question or situation that may occur. To delay or ponder for very long over what to say may create an awkward void in the flow of classroom events that can, and often does, result in a loss of momentum and problems in classroom management (Emmer, Evertson, & Worsham, 2003). But even more important, the momentum of the classroom must be maintained with responses and interactions that satisfy student needs and instructional goals. Few reactions or responses of the teacher can be put off until tomorrow, until the end of the period, or even for a minute. Most of the queries, questions, and solicitations made by students need immediate responses if they are to be effective in satisfying student needs. This makes practically every exchange a test of the teacher's responsiveness. It also tests the teacher's skill at keeping the flow going in ways that respond to, rather than put off, student needs for information, clarification, or further discussion.

Interruption

Think back to some of your experiences as a student. How often were classroom routines interrupted by an unexpected announcement from the office or someone at the door? A third characteristic of classroom life that you will notice is the number of times the natural flow of the classroom is interrupted. A source of frustration for most teachers, such events can so alter the momentum within a classroom that both student achievement and classroom discipline can be affected by them. Perhaps in no other profession are individuals interrupted so frequently in the course of delivering or providing a message than in teaching. Even unsolicited salespeople generally are allowed to complete their message—and who ever heard of a surgeon being interrupted during an operation by a messenger at the door! Messengers, public address bulletins, students straggling in late for class, changing course schedules, getting parent signatures, and making announcements are only some of the many interruptions that invade the instructional routine of daily classroom life. As even your earliest classroom observations will reveal, teachers do a lot more than teach, and sometimes are interrupted more than they teach. Being able to see the many types of interruptions that occur in classrooms and how effective and ineffective teachers manage these interruptions is another important skill for observation—and for teaching.

Social Dynamics

The fourth characteristic of a classroom is its social dynamics. Let's not forget: teaching is a group process. Even in one-on-one encounters, students are aware of other members of the group, and so rarely perceive themselves as individuals in the classroom. As a result, teachers confront many important instructional and management decisions related to group dynamics (Borich, 2004, chapters 9 & 10).

In order to capitalize on the positive aspects of group membership and encourage a sense of inclusion, many teachers implement discussion sessions, student teams, small groups, and the sharing of instructional materials to create opportunities for positive social interaction among their students. But learning in groups can also create opportunities for social distraction—which may dampen the learning process. Friends and enemies are often found in the same class, and excitement and expectations that often start outside class are easily carried into the classroom. There is, in other words, ample opportunity for groups in school to behave as groups do outside of school, with all the same characteristics: jealousies, competition, playfulness, laughter, and argument. Although common outside the classroom, these characteristics can create social distraction and off-task behavior within the classroom. Few professions require their members to work in such a confined space with so many individuals for so long a time during the day as does teaching. Add to this scene the fact that some individuals do not want to be there, and you have the perfect social setting for learners to become distracted by one another. The teacher's ability to plan and carry out activities that promote cooperative interaction and discourage social distraction can make the difference between an effective and an ineffective classroom. Observing the social dynamics of classrooms will help you discover what types of activities minimize social distraction and maximize cooperative interaction among students. It will also help you understand how and why teachers can sometimes be unaware of how their own behavior contributes to or detracts from establishing a cooperative and cohesive learning environment that includes rather than distances learners.

BECOMING AWARE OF CLASSROOM BEHAVIOR: LENSES FOR SELF-IMPROVEMENT

Given the rapidity, immediacy, interruption, and social dynamics of classrooms, it is easy to see why teachers are busy people. Few occupations could boast of having a thousand or more interactions with clients or customers in a single day, yet teachers customarily do this not just for one day, but for practically every day of the school year. Add to this the fact that the teacher's job is to facilitate the learning of subject matter content and to determine that what is taught is learned, and we have a particularly demanding job. The effect of this ambitious undertaking is that most of a teacher's attention is focused on the subject matter and the students rather than on him or herself. Within the busy schedule of a school day, teachers do not have many opportunities to reflect on the relative merits of the strategies and methods they use. To pause for contemplation during instruction could disrupt the rapidity of classroom events, and almost surely would result in a loss of momentum; to pause after class or at the end of the school day would require the ability to accurately recall events that may have occurred hours earlier. As a result, teachers frequently can be observed performing behaviors that are unintentional and that they are unaware of, such as dominating discussions and allowing too little response time for students to think through an answer, staying with or encouraging answers from high-ability students more than low-ability students, calling on members of one sex more than the other, giving preferential treatment to high-achieving students and more frequently criticizing the wrong answers from low-achieving students, and responding to students from various cultures and linguistic backgrounds differently than to those from the teacher's own background. These behaviors have been observed even among experienced teachers, suggesting that at least some teachers may be so involved in conveying their subject matter content that they are unconscious of many of their own patterns of interaction.

A second reason teachers may be unaware of their teaching behavior is that they are not always given specific signs that define "good" teaching. Broad indexes of effectiveness, such as the number of students completing homework, high grades on classroom quizzes, accumulated points for work completed, and improvement from year to year on standardized tests, are often used to gauge progress within a classroom. Although these are convenient end products of individual student progress, their disadvantage for determining a teacher's effectiveness is that many factors other than the instruction being provided can contribute to them—student motivation, aptitude, past achievement, learning readiness, and home life, to name only a few. Also, since end products often result from many different instructional activities over an extended period of time, they rarely point explicitly to what should be changed to improve the quality of the outcome, and therefore provide little corrective value for changing teacher behavior.

Without clear signs of what to look for to evaluate their teaching, and without the time to consider and reflect on classroom events, many teachers fail to adequately consider their teaching behavior. Thus, focused observation activities and accompanying observation tools are needed to help you develop professional "lenses" for observing others, as well as for assessing your own development as a teacher. A detailed presentation of these professional lenses and tools for observation can be found in *Observation Skills for Effective Teaching,* 4th edition (Borich, 2003). Below we will present a brief introduction and synthesis of them.

As you learn to observe through these lenses, you will want to work toward four major goals: (1) to become aware of your own teaching behavior; (2) to discover alternative instructional practices and new solutions to instructional problems; (3) to learn your personal teaching strengths; and (4) to focus your reflections on important areas of teacher growth and effectiveness. Let's look at each of these goals for classroom observation.

To Become Aware of Your Own Behavior

Although teachers make many decisions each day about the instructional process (how to capture student attention, who they will call on, how they will structure the content, how to summarize the lesson, how misbehavior will be handled, what seatwork to assign, etc.), they sometimes make these decisions unconsciously in the course of meeting the demands of the classroom. They may become bound by routine, failing to recognize how easily decisions can be altered. Instead of being pulled along unconsciously by the stream of rapidly paced events in the classroom, teachers can and should be active decision makers who influence the quality and nature of events in the classroom. They should actively question their own assumptions, and seek input from parents and others on a regular basis (Compton-Lilly, 2000). As you observe in classrooms, you will become aware that the stream of events is not the same in every classroom, and that sometimes teachers make decisions simply out of habit. If your observations lead to questions such as "Should I be doing that?", "Could that work in my classroom?", or "Would I have done that?", your observations are beginning to make you more aware of your own teaching. That awareness can help you discover some of your own unconscious decisions and unchecked assumptions. Even after you complete your university preparation, taking the opportunity to observe others will help remind you of your own behaviors—and how they may appear to others.

To Discover Alternative Instructional Practices and New Solutions to Instructional Problems

Another goal for focused observation is to seek information and example behavior related to a specific area of interest. While each of us has experienced a number of instructional methods and practices as a student, there are many we did not experience—or that we experienced in a limited context. As you enter the teaching profession, it is natural to wonder about new instructional practices, methods, and strategies, and whether new and different educational ideas will help you become a more effective teacher. As you read textbooks, observe other teachers, and practice teach, you'll develop questions about the "how-to's" of teaching. Whether the basis of your curiosity stems from wondering about your own experiences as a student, from wanting to see some textbook procedure come alive in the classroom, or from having experienced a seemingly intractable problem in your own teaching, observation of other classrooms is often a practical solution for discovering and applying new ideas. For example, as you watch a teacher lead a class discussion, you may wonder how a teacher can successfully blend fact- and concept-type questions in the midst of the same discussion. Or you may encounter a problem with misbehavior in your own classroom and want to learn more about the variety of rules used by other teachers for keeping students from calling out without being acknowledged. Focused observations can be among the most rewarding, because they occur in response to an immediate need that has some sense of urgency for your thinking—and later, for your teaching.

To Determine Your Personal Teaching Strengths

Aside from helping you find solutions to instructional problems, focused observation helps put your personal teaching strengths in perspective. Teachers do not always see that a decision they have made, either consciously or unconsciously, could solve an instructional problem of another teacher. This may be due to the fact that many teachers rarely observe others and do not have sufficient opportunities to describe to others the positive achievements in their own classrooms. As you observe, you will discover areas where *your* knowledge and experience provide insights that can help other teachers address a particular challenge. Taking the opportunity to share insights about successes and challenges builds a healthy sense of competence and shared professionalism. This benefit alone is why so many career-ladder and professional development programs require peer observation.

To Focus Your Reflections on Important Areas of Teacher Effectiveness

Handbooks and reviews of classroom research, such as those by Banks and Banks (2001), Brophy (2002), and Richardson (2001) summarize the results of more than twenty-five years of research in classrooms. In these and related texts (Borich, 2004; 2003; Borich & Tombari, 2004, 1997; Cantrell, 1998/1999; Taylor, Pearson, Clark, & Walpole, 1999), the processes used by teachers to instruct students (for example, activity structures, questioning strategies, methods of organizing content) are related to student outcomes (such as engagement in the learning process and performance on classroom and standardized tests). This research has identified effective teaching behaviors related to: (a) the learning climate of a classroom; (b) classroom management; (c) lesson clarity; (d) instructional variety; (e) teacher's task orientation; (f) students' engagement in the learning process; (g) students' success; and (h) students' higher thought processes and performance outcomes.

PART III: APPLICATIONS

LENSES FOR VIEWING CLASSROOM BEHAVIOR

Because classrooms are busy and complex, observers often choose a particular professional frame-or lens-to gain insight regarding a particular aspect of classroom life. Over time, observations are completed using different lenses, resulting in a more comprehensive and detailed understanding of teaching and learning. While the lenses we will use are not the only ones that could guide observation in classrooms, each has been researched and has been found to influence the performance of learners. Other lenses for viewing classroom behavior are also available, and new lenses will undoubtedly emerge from classroom research in the future. For our purposes, the following lenses will serve as an introduction to acquiring classroom observation skills and beginning to teach effectively.

Area 1: Consider the Learning Climate

The **learning climate** of a classroom refers to its physical and emotional environment. Some observable features of the learning environment are (a) the warmth, concerns, and expectations conveyed to students by the teacher; (b) the organization of the physical aspects of the classroom, which promotes or precludes cohesion and interaction among students; and (c) the competitiveness, cooperation, or independence encouraged by the structure of activity within the classroom.

As you observe the learning climate of a classroom, you will want to note how students feel about themselves, about one another, and about their classroom, and the activities and materials that promote feelings most conducive to learning.

Area 2: Focus on Classroom Management

Classroom management involves how teachers organize the classroom and anticipate and respond to student behavior to provide an environment for efficient learning. Some observable features of classroom management are organizing the physical aspects of the classroom to match instructional goals; preestablishing and communicating classroom rules; developing and communicating instructional routines; establishing a system of incentives and consequences; and using techniques for low-profile classroom management. Because many beginning teachers find effective classroom management challenging, you'll want to pay close attention to how effective teachers orchestrate and facilitate learning with their classroom management skills.

Area 3: Look for Lesson Clarity

Lesson clarity refers to a teacher's ability to speak clearly and directly, and to organize and structure content at the students' current level of understanding. Some observable features of lesson clarity are informing learners of expected skills and understandings before a lesson; providing advance organizers that place the lesson content in the perspective of past and future learning; reviewing and summarizing; and using examples, illustrations, demonstrations and instructional media that can expand and clarify lesson content.

Area 4: Verify Variety

As you recall from your own experiences as a student, **instructional variety**, using different modes of learning (visual, oral, and tactile) maintains interest and attention. Effective teachers select an appropriate mix of instructional approaches to support particular learning objectives. Some observable features of instructional variety are the use of attention-gaining devices; variation in eye contact, voice, and gestures; use of alternate modes through which learning is to occur (seeing, listening, and doing); and using appropriate rewards and reinforcers to sustain student interest and engagement.

Area 5: Observe Task Orientation

Task orientation involves effective teaching practices that help the teacher maintain an instructional focus. It includes managing classroom activities efficiently; handling misbehavior with minimum disruption to the class; reducing instructional time devoted to clerical duties; and maximizing time devoted to content coverage. Some of the most observable features of task orientation are lesson plans that reflect the text and curriculum guide, use of rules and procedures that anticipate and thereby reduce misbehavior, and established milestones (for example, tests, reviews, and assignments) for maintaining instructional momentum.

Area 6: Examine Engagement

Students learn best when they become actively engaged in the learning process. Teachers promote **student engagement** by providing exercises, problem sets, and activities that allow students to think about, act on, and practice what they learn. Some observable features of teachers facilitating student engagement in the learning process are the provision of activities for guided practice; the use of feedback and correctives; the use of individualized and self-directed learning activities; the systematic use of meaningful verbal praise; and checking and monitoring of classroom assignments during seatwork.

Area 7: Measure Student Success

Students' learning is enhanced when they complete work at moderate to high levels of success. Some of the most observable features of teaching that promote **student success** are unit and lesson organization that reflects prior learning; immediate feedback and corrections; gradual transitions to new content; and a classroom pace and momentum that builds toward major milestones (for example, reviews, projects, practice exercises, and tests).

Area 8: Look for Higher Thought Processes and Performance Outcomes

Higher thought processes include decision-making, problem-solving, critical thinking, and valuing behaviors that alone cannot be measured by standardized tests of cognitive achievement. Some observable features of teaching for higher thought processes are using collaborative and group activities; demonstrating mental models and strategies for learning; arranging for student projects and demonstrations; engaging students in oral performance; providing opportunities for independent practice; and using performance assessments and student portfolios.

Although you will want to observe classrooms with specific questions or goals, your first few observations may be more general so that you can get a feel for particular grade levels or schools. These eight professional lenses can be used to help you consider the overall picture of a classroom. To see how all eight lenses can work together to inform your observation and suggest specific questions for further study, let's visit a fictional classroom taught by Ms. Koker. Before we begin, look over the eight professional lenses for focused observation below. Then, when you are finished reading about the events in Ms. Koker's classroom, complete the *General Observation Form* below to rate her classroom on each of our eight professional lenses.

General Observation Form

Instructions: On the blank for each lens place a check mark, closest to the word that best describes the classroom you are observing.

Learning Climate

Teacher Centered __ __ __ __ __ __ __ Student Centered

Classroom Management

Orderly __ __ __ __ __ __ __ Disorderly

Lesson Clarity

Clear __ __ __ __ __ __ __ Unclear

Instructional Variety

Varied __ __ __ __ __ __ __ Static

Teacher's Task Orientation

Focused __ __ __ __ __ __ __ Unfocused

	Students' Engagement in the Learning Process
	Students Students Involved __ __ __ __ __ __ __Uninvolved
	Students' Success in Basic Academic Skills
	High __ __ __ __ __ __ __ Low
	Higher Thought Processes & Performance Outcomes
	Many __ __ __ __ __ __ __ Few

Source: From Borich, G. (2003). *Observation Skills for Effective Teaching*, 4th edition. Upper Saddle River, NJ: Merrill/Prentice Hall. Reprinted with permission.

A CLASSROOM DIALOGUE

The scene is a middle school social studies classroom. Ms. Koker is beginning a unit on forms of government. It is early in the school year, so the class is still new to her. The first several weeks of school were a bit rough for Ms. Koker because she was somewhat unprepared for the aggressive talking-out behavior of some of the students, and because of the new textbook, which devotes less time to some of her favorite topics. Things have calmed down somewhat now that Ms. Koker has established some classroom rules and has decided to organize her lessons more tightly with questions and recitation. Ms. Koker's goals for this lesson are to introduce three types of government, and then begin to develop the concept of democracy. Aside from a tendency to be loud and talkative, this class is composed of mostly average-performing students, with a few who are high-performing and a few who regularly challenge her authority.

Ms. Koker: Today we begin a unit on various forms of government. In the next few days, we will study the concepts of monarchy, oligarchy, and democracy, and how governments are formed using each of these three concepts. In fact, we will cover these three forms of government so thoroughly that at the end of the week, each of you will know how to create a government of your own using each—but, please, don't start any revolutions with what you learn! [Class laughs.] Let's start by defining what a monarchy is. Does anybody know? [At this point, some class members turn to their neighbors to ask if they know the answer.]

Ms. Koker: Please, no talking. Bobby, do you know what a monarchy is?

Bobby: No.

Ms. Koker: Christina, do you have any idea?

Christina: No, I'm afraid I don't, Ms. Koker.

Ms. Koker: Tim, you're not in your seat, so I'll have to ask you. Do you know what a monarchy is?

Tim: Yep, it's a butterfly. [Class bursts out in laughter.]

Ms. Koker: That's an extra assignment for you tonight. Okay, I'll tell you. A monarchy is a government that is ruled or governed by a single person. It's a form of government in which a single person, a king or queen for example, is the supreme head of a state for his or her entire lifetime. Now, what other names besides "King" or "Queen" do we have for individuals who serve as head of a country for a lifetime? Let's go from left to right across the first row.

Mary: I'm not sure what you mean, Ms. Koker.

Ms. Koker: Next. Felipe?

Felipe : You mean, what do we call someone who is just like a king, but called something else?

Ms. Koker: You're on the right track. Next. Anna?

Anna: Well, I would call a king an emperor.

Tim: [Talking out] Yeah, like in "The Emperor's New Clothes!" [Class laughs.]

Ms. Koke:r Okay, that's the second time you've spoken out of turn, Tim. You will answer two extra homework questions tonight if you don't want me to write up a detention slip. Now, go up and write your name on the board, so I won't forget to give you the assignment. [By now, talking has grown louder and a few students have left their seats waiting for Tim to return from the board.] Let's see now, where were we?

Student: [From somewhere in back of room] We were talking about emperors.

Ms. Koker: Yes, emperors, like kings, usually indicate a monarchy— or rule by a single person over a long time. Other names for heads of state that indicate a monarchy are *czar*, which was a title once used in Russia; *kaiser*, which was a term used in the early German empire; and *sultan*, which is a word still used today in the Middle East. These individuals, like kings and emperors throughout history, have often had absolute power over the people and lands they ruled. Traditionally, these rulers gained their power from the family they were born into, and not from any accomplishments of their own. In some cases today, a type of monarchy exists alongside some other form of government. Can anyone think of a country like our own that has a king or a queen? Let's go across the second row this time. Rashaun?

Rashaun: England. They have a queen and royal weddings and that kind of stuff that we don't have in this country.

Ms. Koker: Good, Rashaun. Some present-day monarchs, like the Queen of England, still exist. However, in England the queen possesses only minor authority and exists for mostly symbolic purposes, or as a way of showing the country's historical roots. Although kings and queens did at one time have absolute authority over England, today they serve mostly ceremonial functions. That was a good response, Rashaun. Now, before we move to another form of government, called an oligarchy, does everyone understand what a monarchy is? [No one responds.]

Ms. Koker: Okay, I guess we can go on. Let's see, where did we leave off in the second row? [Tricia meekly raises her hand.] Can you tell us what an oligarchy is, Tricia?

Tricia: I don't know.

Ms. Koker: Next. Raul?

Raul: Don't know.

Ms. Koker: Well, I guess I'll have to tell you—but it's in the chapter, which you should have read. An oligarchy is a form of government in which absolute power or authority is given to a few persons, instead of a single ruler as in a monarchy. These individuals usually come to power not through heredity or being born into the right families, but through some political struggle or compromise. Oligarchies, which were common in ancient times, are hard to find today, but some governments almost like an oligarchy still exist. Can anyone think of one? Jeff, Kathy, you're the last two in the second row. Any ideas?

Jeff : I'm not sure, but is it like a mother and father in a family?

Ms. Koker: What do you mean?

Jeff : Well, my parents have a kind of agreement—not written or anything like that—in which my mother is responsible for taking care of the house and my brothers and sisters, and my father is responsible for his job and doing repairs. That's a kind of sharing of responsibility, isn't it?

Ms. Koker: Yes, maybe. But it's not what we're talking about here. Kathy?

Kathy: I can't think of any examples.

Ms. Koker: Well, ancient Greece was ruled for a brief time by a group of persons called the Thirty Tyrants. This may have been the very first oligarchy. Also, we've been hearing a lot lately about a country called Yugoslavia. In that country power and authority used to be divided among individuals representing each of the states or regions. Now, let's compare the two forms of government we've been discussing—monarchy and oligarchy—with our own form of government. First, let's remind ourselves of what our form of government is called. Let's pick up with the first person in the third row. Quann?

Quann: I'm not ready.

Ms. Koker: Everyone should be ready when I call on them.

Quann: Well, I didn't get to read this yet. [Class begins to snicker at Quann getting in trouble.]

Ms. Koker: Okay, I'm going to make the rule that everyone must read the whole assignment before we begin a topic. That means that the reading for the entire week must be done by class on Monday. [Loud moans are heard.]

Tim: [Speaking without acknowledgment] But that means we'd have homework over the weekend, and no other teacher makes us do that.

Ms. Koker: [Ignoring Tim's comment] We still have one more form of government to discuss. Joan is next. [Class becomes noisy and restless at the thought of weekend homework.]

Joan: We live in a democracy.

Ms. Koker: What else can you tell us about a democracy?

Joan: Well . . . [Just as she is about to begin, the public address system clicks on.]

Principal: [On P.A.] I'm sorry to interrupt, but two lunchtime jobs are still available for any students who want to be paid for working in the cafeteria during the second half of their lunch. We need some workers for today, so, teachers, if anyone is interested, please write them a hall permit and send them to the office immediately. Thank you. [Roberto and Tim raise their hands, indicating their interest in the job. The teacher ignores Tim and writes a pass to the office for Roberto.]

Ms. Koker: Okay, we were discussing democracy. Time is short, so take out paper and pen and write down everything I say. Another rule we will start tomorrow, since you're not doing the reading, is to take notes on everything I say. The word *democracy* comes from the Greek word *demos*, which means "the people," and the Greek word *kratein*, spelled K-R-A-T-E-I-N, which means "to rule."

Brittany: [Calling out] How is that first word spelled?

Ms. Koker: [Responds by spelling the word.] D-E-M-O-S. So, who's next to be called on? [Rhonda raises her hand.] Okay. Rhonda, putting these two words together, what does the word *democracy* mean?

Rhonda: It means that the people rule.

Ms. Koker: Good. And who are the people in a democracy? Sam?

Sam I guess it's all of us—everyone that lives in a certain place.

Ms. Koker: Okay, a democracy differs from a monarchy and an oligarchy by who is given the authority to rule. As we have seen, in a monarchy, a single person, usually chosen through heredity, is given absolute authority, and in the case of an oligarchy, a small number of persons, representing only a fraction of all the people in the land, are given the authority to rule. In a democracy authority to rule rests in the hands of all the people. But how could such a system work when everyone has authority over everyone else? Next person. Diana?

Diana: We—or I should say all the people—elect persons to represent us. I guess that's what our senators and representatives do.

Ms. Koker: So when we say that all the people have the authority to rule in a democracy, we really mean . . . Next. That's you, Phil.

Phil: We elect persons—like Diana said—representatives and senators, and we give them the authority to rule.

Ms. Koker: Yes. So in a democracy like ours, the people have authority, but indirectly, through the election of individuals that represent their interests. In our form of democracy, called *representative democracy*, a legislature composed of senators and representatives is elected by the people. Does anyone know of any other kind of democracy? Mark, you're next.

Mark: Nope.

Ms. Koker: Did you take notes on the chapter?

Mark: I was going to do that tonight.

Ms. Koker: I will begin checking notes at the end of every class. Since some of you haven't read the assignment, we'll use the remaining time to read Chapter 7.

Reactions From Observing Ms. Koker's Classroom

Although this dialogue may not have been fair to Ms. Koker's everyday teaching, classroom exchanges such as this occur at almost all levels of schooling. They are, to be sure, uneven, rough, and sometimes even crude attempts to convey information in the midst of all sorts of competing forces—misbehaving and unprepared students, interruptions, quickly sketched lesson plans, and insufficient instructional time, to name only a few. The flow of events in a classroom, as shown in the dialogue, is not always a neatly packaged, smooth unit of instruction. Instead, teachers and students often struggle, sometimes with themselves and sometimes with each other, to complete the day's lesson. Although Ms. Koker's classroom may have had some problems, these problems are not uncommon for any teacher at one time or another.

Think back for a moment on the dialogue you have just read. In your opinion, was it an example of effective teaching or ineffective teaching, or did it contain some examples of each? What are your impressions of Ms. Koker as a person and as a teacher? What about her knowledge and use of instructional methods? Did she do the right things most of the time, even though not all the students conveniently cooperated, or did some of her decisions make it less likely that the goals of the lesson would be achieved? Do you believe the goals for this lesson, as stated before the dialogue, were met? If not, whose fault was it—Ms. Koker's, for not motivating the students; the students', for not reading the assignment; Tim's, for misbehaving; or the principal's, for creating a distraction at a crucial time?

Of course, all of these factors and others were instrumental in the way life in this classroom unfolded. But if we were to attempt to fully understand life in this classroom, each of the questions we asked ourselves would point us in equally narrow, and perhaps even biased, directions. A broader set of lenses than individual questions or idiosyncratic concerns that happen to gain our attention would be necessary to view classroom life. As you consider the interactions in Ms. Koker's classroom, look over the *General Observation Form* and complete your rating for each of our eight professional lenses for focused observation.

In what areas did you notice positive interactions? In what areas do you feel concern? Did seeing the observation form earlier help you "observe" Ms. Koker and her students more effectively?

The eight areas of effective teaching can help us achieve the breadth of vision we need to understand the events in Ms. Koker's classroom. Let's use each of these "professional frames" as a lens to achieve a more focused observation of life in Ms. Koker's classroom. After viewing the events through each of these lenses, we will bring all our data together to form some general impressions of the strengths and weaknesses of Ms. Koker's presentation. As you read the following discussion, add any notes to your *General Observation Form* that may help you remember key points about each of the eight lenses.

Consider the Learning Climate

Recall that the learning climate of a classroom involves the social and emotional environment in which learning takes place. Some of the most noticeable features of a learning climate are the warmth, concerns, and expectations conveyed to students by the teacher; the organization of the physical aspects of the classroom that promote or preclude cohesion and interaction among students; and the competitiveness, cooperation, or independence encouraged by the teacher's instructional routine. Using these aspects of the learning environment as our lens, let's look back at the dialogue to see how the learning climate may have influenced the achievement of Ms. Koker's goals for the lesson.

In many ways, the learning climate in Ms. Koker's classroom appears tense. On one hand, Ms. Koker seems genuinely committed to having students contribute their ideas to the development of the concepts she is teaching. But, on the other hand, few students seem to feel free or relaxed enough to share anything but the most obvious answers. As a result, very little genuine discussion takes place.

The manner in which Ms. Koker responds to students may also have increased the tension in the classroom. Rarely is an answer followed by another question to the same student. In the case of an inaccurate answer or no answer, the teacher quickly moves to the next student instead of staying with the student to correct a partially wrong answer, or drawing out a partially correct response that another student might build on. Even when opportunities present themselves to stay with a student and develop his or her response further, such as when Jeff equates the sharing of responsibilities among members of an oligarchy with the sharing of responsibilities between his mother and father, the teacher responds with a curt "But it's not what we're talking about here." These moves on the part of Ms. Koker enhance the competitive nature of this classroom by treating each individual student response as either all right or all wrong, thereby missing the opportunity to connect the discussion to the students' own experiences.

Another aspect of the tense learning climate results from Ms. Koker's desire to keep firm control of the events occurring in her classroom. Ms. Koker decided on a carefully controlled row-by-row recitation of answers instead of an open discussion. Perhaps in an effort to enhance classroom management, she restricts any interaction that is not a direct response to her questions. Consequently, she restricts the very type of response that her discussion-oriented agenda seems to call for. Without realizing it, Ms. Koker sets up a learning climate of opposing forces. The students resist being drawn into the discussion to avoid saying anything unacceptable; the teacher asks for student participation but responds with mostly unrewarding answers. Had the atmosphere of the classroom been less rigid, this class might have been more conducive to the cooperative interchanges being sought by the teacher. Now let's get a feel for some of the other lenses through which life in Ms. Koker's classroom can be observed.

Focus on Classroom Management

What did you notice about Ms. Koker's classroom management style? Did it appear to be more of a reaction to student behavior than a well-organized system of rules and procedures thought out in advance? At several points in the lesson, Ms. Koker seems to make up rules on the spot. Although sometimes necessary, this practice is risky. It can convey to students a sense of arbitrariness about the rule itself, making it seem less credible, and therefore less likely to be obeyed. Apparently, Ms. Koker failed to convey some basic rules earlier in the school year (for example, when to complete assigned reading and take notes). Without a well-organized system of rules and class procedures, Ms. Koker may continue to react defensively, at first tolerating a wide range of behavior, and later using valuable class time pulling back to respond to behaviors she didn't foresee.

Ms. Koker's classroom also exhibits problems with conduct. Talking out, for which presumably a rule was communicated earlier, seems to be a persistent problem. This comes as no surprise, because Ms. Koker's response to talking out, even in this short episode, was inconsistent. Notice that Ms. Koker is adamant at first about not speaking out. After reminding the class at the beginning of the lesson, "Please, no talking out," and reprimanding Tim for talking out, she accepts without reprimand a call out from an anonymous student. After which she switches unexpectedly to a nondirective style ("Let's see now, where were we?") more suited to an informal discussion session than the row-by-row recitation format she had pursued from the beginning of the lesson.

Did you also notice the amount of class time and resulting problems created by Ms. Koker's response to Tim's misbehavior? Although

Tim's misbehavior might have been unpredictable, Ms. Koker's response to it may have created an even bigger problem. First, she responds by assigning extra homework, thereby equating homework with punishment. Second, during the time it took for Tim to leave his seat, go to the board to write his name, and return, the rest of the class waited without direction. The momentum, or pace, which previously kept the class moving forward and focused on the lesson, was lost. These momentary lapses, whether due to interruptions from misbehaving students, public address announcements, or visitors at the door, require special classroom management procedures to keep students engaged in the learning process. Ms. Koker's use of instructional time for discipline might have been avoided had she established and consistently reinforced an organized system of classroom rules and procedures from the start of the school year.

Looking for Lesson Clarity

Lesson clarity involves communicating clearly and directly, and presenting content at the students' current level of understanding. Clarity involves not only the visual and oral clarity of a teacher's delivery, but also the proper organization and structuring of the material to be taught. For example, to organize and structure the material to be taught, the teacher must know how much knowledge the students already have about the day's lesson. Notice that Ms. Koker begins the lesson by saying, "Let's start by defining what a monarchy is. Does anybody know?" The responses she receives, however, are not too encouraging. The first two students called on say no, after which Ms. Koker says, "I guess I'll have to tell you then" This beginning involves two aspects of clarity: checking for relevant prior knowledge, and summarizing or reviewing when it is discovered that the students do not have the knowledge necessary to understand the day's lesson. Had Ms. Koker not discovered early in the lesson that students had little or no knowledge of the day's topic, she might have gone on to more advanced concepts, never realizing her students did not have a basis for understanding the material she was presenting. As it was, most of the lesson seemed to cover the basics of what the students should have already learned from reading the text. Phrases such as "Okay, I'll tell you" and "It's in the chapter" are clues that not all of the class may have read the assignment, leading Ms. Koker to make explicit a rule that, in the future, all assigned reading be completed before a topic is discussed in class.

Some other aspects of clarity involve informing the students of the skills or understanding expected at the end of the lesson, and organizing the content for future lessons. Recall that, to some extent, Ms. Koker's opening remark reflects both these aspects of clarity. The students are informed of the three forms of government to be covered, and are told that they are expected to know how to form the three types of government at the end of the unit. Both of these ingredients of the day's lesson worked to make Ms. Koker's lesson more understandable.

Verifying Instructional Variety

Another lens through which to observe Ms. Koker's classroom is instructional variety. Instructional variety includes the varied use of rewards, reinforcements, and types of questions asked (for example, recall vs. application), as well as the teacher's use of instructional media to enhance student attention and engagement with the lesson. It also involves the flexibility of the teacher to change strategies or shift directions when needed. Variety can be enhanced by a teacher's animation (through variation in eye contact, voice, and gestures), as well as through the use of different instructional strategies and media within the same lesson. We did not see Ms. Koker teaching, but from what we read, there seems to have been little variety to her lesson. She persists with her questioning technique, even though she seems to have little success with it, until finally, out of necessity, she assumes a more direct lecture approach at the end of the lesson. Also, her questions call only for basic facts and definitions: "What is a monarchy?" and "Can you tell us what an oligarchy is?" instead of "What are its advantages and disadvantages?", "How is it formed?'', or "What lessons can we learn from these three forms of government for governing ourselves?" Focusing only on factual recall may fail to engage some students in the learning process.

Instructional variety is also achieved by choosing specific activity structures to convey lesson content. The term **activity structure** refers both to how the students are organized for learning and how the lesson is organized. Both categories of structure appear in Ms. Koker's classroom. For example, we note that Ms. Koker chooses to organize her instruction around student recitation in an almost drill-and-practice format. We noted previously the possible mismatch between such a format and what appears to be the discussion-oriented goal of her lesson. At that time, we suspected that this structure was selected more as a way to manage classroom talk than as an effective vehicle for achieving the goals of the lesson. The choice of a recitation format led Ms. Koker to call on students one by one in a predesignated order, as might be done if students were giving their answers orally to questions from a workbook. The results were factual responses that avoided any risk on the part of the students, rather than the type of responses that could result in more complex or integrated learning.

Observing the Teacher's Task Orientation

Teacher's task orientation is the percentage of time allocated to a lesson in which the teacher is actually teaching material related to the topic. In the dialogue, attention to the misbehavior of individual students, time spent introducing new rules about conduct and academic work, and interruption from the school administrator all took their toll on the time that could have been devoted to instruction. As a result of these interruptions, the time Ms. Koker actually spent teaching the content was limited. When teachers inefficiently handle misbehavior or spend large amounts of class time doing clerical chores (for example, passing out papers, stapling and collating, reprimanding misbehaving students) which may be done more efficiently in other ways or at other times, instructional time may be only a small percentage of the total amount of time allocated to the lesson. Although we have no way of knowing the exact amount of time Ms. Koker's instruction was interrupted by noninstructional demands, a simple count of the total number of lines of dialogue minus the number of lines containing dialogue *unrelated* to the goals of the lesson reveals that about 34 percent of Ms. Koker's teaching was off-task. If this continued throughout the school day, more than 18 minutes of every hour would be devoted to noninstructional events.

Noninstructional events that compete for instructional time include formulating classroom rules, giving directives, administering reprimands, dealing with interruptions, creating orderly transitions between subjects or activities, and engaging in activities that structure the learning environment. The amount of time actually devoted to instruction often depends on how efficiently noninstructional activities are managed. Poor classroom management can detract from time spent on instructional tasks, decreasing students' engagement in the learning process and, predictably, interfering with success in completing assignments correctly. Although we saw only a brief view of Ms. Koker's classroom, she made some important decisions about classroom rules, the use of reinforcement, and the handling of misbehavior that affected the amount of time devoted to instruction during this lesson.

Examining Students' Engagement in the Learning Process

A sixth lens through which to observe a lesson is student engagement in the learning process. Like the task orientation of a teacher, this behavior is often measured as a percentage of time. Student engagement in the learning process pertains to the percentage of time the teacher presents instructionally relevant content (is task oriented) *and* the students are acting on, thinking about, or otherwise using the content being taught. In contrast to a teacher's task orientation, a student's engagement in the learning process may be much more difficult to determine. A student may look attentive or appear to be working through the workbook, but her thoughts may be miles away. In the example, part of the time Ms. Koker was teaching, at least some of her students were not engaged in the learning process.

By relying on individual recitation, Ms. Koker does little to involve students in the lesson. Aside from her questions and a few attempts to reward a correct answer with praise, Ms. Koker seems to encourage only a passive or mechanical involvement in the lesson. Absent from Ms. Koker's lesson is a broad range of questions that might excite the imagination of students and encourage them to keep trying after a wrong answer or no answer. Perhaps most relevant to the apparent disengagement of some of the students was Ms. Koker's drill-and-practice style, which requires students to respond in order across rows. This ordered-turns approach is often recommended for content in which many discrete pieces of knowledge with clearly defined right and wrong answers is being recalled. But Ms. Koker's content seems concept-oriented. After a time, students in the back half of the room could pretty much guarantee that they would not get called on during the class, providing even more opportunity for these students to disengage from the learning process. This, together with Ms. Koker's sometimes critical responses to a wrong answer or no answer, may have provided a reason for those who had already responded to turn their attention elsewhere. If more complicated and time-consuming responses were being sought, it may have been better for Ms. Koker to call on students who volunteered and who, therefore, may have provided answers around which she could have built lesson content. Ms. Koker could also have implemented any of a number of cooperative group activities to encourage greater student participation.

Measuring Student Success

What signs of student success did you see in Ms. Koker's classroom? Student success pertains to the percentage of correct responses given to classroom questions, class exercises, and workbook assignments. When an expository or didactic approach (which seems to fit Ms. Koker's recitation format) to learning is used, the percentage of student success after the first time through the material should be about 60 to 80 percent to encourage further response and engagement in the learning process. When the success rate is, on the average, less than 60 percent, it may indicate that the lesson content is too difficult or that the exercises are inappropriate for the material being taught. Ultimately, homework and further assignments should work toward creating an average success rate of 90 percent or higher.

Ms. Koker's students seemed reluctant to participate, avoiding, rather than engaging in, the lesson. Students found it safer to say "I don't know" than to risk a wrong or partially wrong response and be criticized for it. Ms. Koker seemed to accept only a narrow definition of correct responses. As a result, the success of her students in answering questions was not very high. Most students avoided answering altogether, and others failed to provide the correct answer. These two student behaviors tell us a lot about Ms. Koker's classroom. Failure to actively involve students in the lesson and present instruction that most students can respond to correctly are indications that the level of the lesson may not have been properly matched to the students' current level of understanding.

As was the case with student engagement, there are certain teacher activities that encourage a moderate to high success rate. These include providing correctives immediately following a wrong or partially right answer, dividing lesson content into small segments at the learner's current level of understanding, planning transitions to new content in small, easy-to-grasp steps, and continually relating the parts of the lesson to larger objectives and goals. Seatwork assigned prior to the day's lesson is one way to check student success rate. If a low success rate is confirmed, Ms. Koker could provide more practice opportunities or cooperative learning activities to actively engage students in the learning process before embarking on the next lesson.

Looking for Higher Thought Processes and Performance Outcomes

The final lens through which to observe Ms. Koker's classroom takes the previous lens, student success, to a higher level. For this lens our focus turns from the recitation of correct responses to higher thought processes, which arise out of teaching and learning activities that promote critical thinking, reasoning, and problem solving. These processes cannot be measured by tests of cognitive achievement alone. The higher thought processes required for analyzing, synthesizing, and decision making in adult contexts are stimulated by interacting with peers and adults and by increasing awareness of one's own learning.

By requiring oral responses, Ms. Koker encourages students to exhibit higher thought processes. But, Ms. Koker fails to follow up on her students' responses and lift them to a higher level. Recall that most of her responses were short and noncorrective, often moving to another student if the response was right, or failing to probe more deeply with another question if the response was incorrect. Ms. Koker saw each answer as either correct or incorrect—not as an opportunity to make a wrong answer right or a good answer better. This left her students responding at the lowest level of behavioral complexity, even though her lesson seemed, at times, aimed at acquiring concepts, patterns of thinking, and judgments.

In other words, Ms. Koker's presentation lacks a plan for helping her students meaningfully learn the content. For example, alerting her students at the start of the lesson to look for some of the features that could distinguish a monarchy from an oligarchy from a democracy might have encouraged her students to analyze the differences between various forms of government, their purposes in history, and advantages or disadvantages in today's world. Although not every lesson need achieve these types of higher thought processes, teachers can and should capitalize on potential opportunities whenever possible.

Also, while student collaboration was not a lesson objective, students collaborating with one another or building on the responses of others could have created classroom interaction that engaged more students and improved student understanding of the concepts being presented. Ms. Koker could have shaped responses in small steps or allowed the thoughts and judgments of individual students to inform the group, so that larger concepts, patterns of thinking, and judgments could have accumulated gradually and cooperatively. By using student responses and collaborative learning activities to encourage problem-solving and judgment skills, routine recitation at the beginning of the class might have turned into higher thought processes by the end of the class.

If you thought our description of Ms. Koker's classroom seemed a bit unfair, you're probably right. A lot happened to Ms. Koker in less time than it generally takes to teach a single lesson. Although our picture of Ms. Koker was compressed for illustrative purposes, teachers at all levels of experience and training are confronted with, and must manage, similar events. Real teachers in real classrooms are never immune from these and similar problems, despite the extent of their training or years of experience.

As we conclude our discussion of Ms. Koker's class, it is important to note the interrelationship among all eight lenses through which we viewed these classroom events. Seldom is the behavior observed under one lens independent of that being observed under others. This reflects the interactive nature of life in classrooms. In other words, if we were to observe Ms. Koker's classroom with only one or even a few of our lenses, an incomplete and possibly distorted observation would result. This is especially obvious when we consider how the learning climate established by Ms. Koker, her classroom management techniques, and the presentation of content all work to influence student behavior. Remember, too, that Ms. Koker's behavior, classroom management style, and presentation were influenced by her students' behavior during the lesson. Thus, it would be futile to separate these interactive aspects of a classroom in real life. Your final goal as an experienced observer is to understand the overall patterns and rhythms of classrooms using all of our lenses.

PART IV: EXTENSIONS

Because systematic observation involves observing and then recording behavioral signs in a form that can be retrieved and studied at a later time, it usually involves a record, or instrument. The instruments used for recording classroom behavior can range from relatively unstructured (taking notes), to highly structured (involving explicit procedures for when and how long to observe specific behaviors). In this section we briefly summarize some of the most frequently used tools to systematically observe and record classroom observations arranged from least structured to most structured. These and other recording formats and observation instruments are described in greater detail and illustrated in *Observation Skills for Effective Teaching,*4th edition (Borich, 2003).

NARRATIVE REPORTS

Narrative reports represent the least structured method of recording classroom observations. Narrative reports do not specify the exact behavioral signs to be observed, but instead simply describe events, in written form, as they occur. Little guidance is given to the observer about what to include or exclude from the observation. Thus, narrative reports are sometimes referred to as *open-ended,* meaning that considerable flexibility about what events to record is given to the observer. You may find it helpful to think of narrative reports as note-taking activities. While there are many ways to take notes, four methods are particularly helpful for classroom observations: anecdotal reports, ethnographic records, thematic notes, and visual maps.

Anecdotal Reports

An **anecdotal report** describes a critical or unusual incident that occurs in the classroom which may be related to an event of larger consequence. It takes the form of a written paragraph that describes what, how, when, and to whom the critical incident happened. Because of the special significance of separating fact from interpretation, anecdotal reports are divided into two distinct parts: (a) facts (for example: "John began reading and the teacher asked him to read louder, saying, 'speak up, or you'll never be good at public speaking'") and (b) an interpretation of the facts (for example: "The teacher's comment to John in front of the class may have reduced his confidence and discouraged others from volunteering"). Anecdotal reports are most useful when they occur over time. For example, after an observer makes an initial interpretation, she returns to the classroom at a later date (perhaps several times) to clarify that interpretation. The focus of later observations is to expand on the interpretation's usefulness and validity.

Ethnographic Records

Ethnographic records report events sequentially, as they occur, without selecting a specific focus or incident. Ethnographic records differ from anecdotal reports in that the observer records a continuous stream of events on a laptop computer, usually for the duration of an entire class period and occasionally longer, and records all the behavior occurring, not just selected incidents. For example:

8:30 Children have just been let into the classroom. Several boys are in the corner fighting and some girls are sitting on the floor playing a puzzle. Teacher and teacher aide are in the back of the room talking.

8:35 Teacher says, "Blue group, get your folders and go up to the front. Green group, come here."

8:38 Noise level drops and children begin to follow directions, etc.

As with anecdotal reports, it is important that the observer record only what is observed, and avoid judgments or interpretations unless they are clearly divided from the factual portion of the record.

Thematic Notes

Thematic notes are facts recorded in traditional outline form, according to predesignated categories of observation. Much like the detective at the scene of a crime who jots down predetermined categories of facts, such as suspects, motives, times, and places, you can use thematic notes to jot down relevant data. Thematic notes can be recorded using Roman numerals (I, II, III, and so on), representing the major areas to be observed, and letters of the alphabet (A, B, C, and so on), representing the factual information observed under each of the more general areas. For example:

I.   Learning Climate

   A. Teacher's exchanges with kids are mostly businesslike.

   B. Atmosphere is competitive as workbooks are being checked.

   C. Teacher evaluates student workbooks orally by using phrases such as: "read over what you've written," "check your work," "follow directions."

To prepare thematic notes, first determine the precise themes or areas on which to focus the observation, and then jot down key facts corresponding to these areas as the action unfolds.

Visual Maps

Visual maps use pictures instead of words to serve much the same purpose as narratives. Visual maps portray the spatial relationships among physical objects—learning centers, reference libraries, groups at work—that may be important to fully understanding anecdotal reports, ethnographic records, or thematic notes. When you observe events that are clearly related to the spatial layout of a classroom, you'll want to construct a visual map to help you (and others) better understand your narrative record. Often, a visual map can help show how a particular instructional activity was implemented, or cooperative activities were organized (for example, how cooperative groups are spaced in the classroom to allow communication between the groups).

RATING SCALES

Narrative reports allow the observer a great deal of flexibility in choosing which behaviors will be observed. On the other hand, rating scales are more structured and offer you the opportunity to record not only what behaviors you observe, but also the degree of the behavior that you note. In order to use a rating scale, you identify, in advance, the behaviors you want to observe. Rating scales can be used individually or in conjunction with other observation tools such as narrative reports. Two common types of rating scale formats are checklists and summated rating scales.

Checklists

The simplest type of rating scale is a **checklist**. Checklists consist of a list of the behaviors to be observed alongside response boxes labeled yes/no or present/absent. Your job as an observer is simply to note the presence or absence of a particular behavior during an observation and mark it on the scale. (For example: Teacher asked higher order questions: Yes ☐ No ☐.) Simple checklists of this sort are most useful when you are observing behaviors that are difficult to evaluate in degree, but that can be identified as either occurring or not occurring.

Summated Rating Scales

Summated ratings differ from checklists in that more than two degrees of discrimination are possible. Summated rating scales help you focus more closely on the degree of behavior because they typically describe a behavior at its extremes and at selected intermediate points. As you observe a behavior, you compare what you observe with the scale and choose the degree or number that best matches your observation. When items represent a common underlying theme, scores across individual scales are summed and averaged, hence the name *summated ratings*. The most common summated rating scales offer five or seven degrees of discrimination. For example: This classroom is:

Teacher centered ___ ___ ___ ___ ___ ___ ___ Student centered

You used a summated rating scale when you completed the *General Observation Form* to assess Ms. Koker's classroom.

CLASSROOM CODING SYSTEMS

Observation systems that help you record the *frequency* with which various teacher and student behaviors occur are called **classroom coding systems**. They are sometimes referred to as low-inference observation systems because they require fewer judgments or inferences on the part of the observer than summated ratings. Unlike the general concepts measured by rating scales, coding systems measure the frequency of specific and distinct units of behavior, such as "Teacher asks questions" or "Teacher used example," that can be tallied during relatively brief intervals of time. One of the most popular observation coding system is called a *counting* system. With a counting system, the observer counts the number of time intervals in which various teacher and/or student behaviors occur. A time interval (such as every five seconds), represents a frame for the observation that is established before the observation begins. Every time the interval or frame elapses, a tally is made to indicate which behavior on the instrument occurred during that interval.

FOR REFLECTION

1. Describe in your own words what a "professional frame" is and give several examples.

2. Of the eight goals for focused observation, what would be two toward which you would work the hardest?

3. Identify four characteristics of classrooms that make them unlike most other work environments.

4. Identify eight professional lenses for observing in classrooms. Describe the behavioral indices you would want to observe for two of them.

5. Using the *General Observation Form* used to observe Ms Koker, what were her strongest and weakest areas?

6. What is the purpose of a narrative report?

7. What are four methods for making a narrative report? Describe how you would record what you see for one of them.

8. How does a checklist differ from a summated rating scale?

9. How is a classroom coding system different from a checklist or summated rating scale?

10. With the help of *Observation Skills for Effective Teaching*, 4th edition, construct an example of a checklist, summated rating scale or classroom coding system for measuring one or more of the eight professional frames for focused observation.

GLOSSARY

activity structure This term refers both to how students are organized for learning and how the lessons are organized.

anecdotal report A form of narrative reporting that describes a critical or unusual incident that occurs in a classroom which may be related to an event of larger consequence.

checklists A list of the behaviors to be observed alongside a yes/no or present/absent response scale.

classroom coding systems Observation systems that record the frequency with which various teacher and student behaviors occur.

classroom management How teachers organize the classroom and anticipate and respond to student behavior to provide an environment for efficient learning.

ethnographic records A form of narrative reporting in which events are recorded sequentially, as they occur, without selecting a specific focus or incident.

higher thought processes Critical thinking, reasoning and problem solving behaviors that alone cannot be measured by formal tests of cognitive achievement.

instructional variety The teacher's use of different modes of learning (visual, oral, and tactile) to maintain interest and attention and promote learning.

Interstate New Teacher Assessment and Support Consortium (INTASC) NBPTS (see below) board compatible standards reviewed by professional organizations and state agencies as a basis for licensing beginning teachers.

learning climate The physical and emotional environment of the classroom indicating its degree of warmth, cohesion, interaction and cooperation.

lesson clarity The teacher's ability to speak clearly and directly to the class, and to organize and structure content at the students' current level of understanding.

National Board for Professional Teaching Standards (NBPTS)
A set of standards prepared mostly by and for teachers indicating what teachers should be able to do along with a voluntary system to certify teachers who meet these standards.

professional frame An objective viewpoint from which to evaluate and act on events critical to becoming an expert.

student engagement The teacher's ability to actively get students to think about, act on, and practice what they learn.

student success Student success pertains to the percentage of correct responses given to classroom questions, class exercises, and workbook assignments. When an expository or didactic approach to learning is used, the percentage of student success after the first time through the material should be about 60 to 80. Ultimately, homework and further assignments should work toward creating an average success rate of 90 percent or higher.

summated rating scales A type of scale in which the observer compares what is observed with what is on the scale and chooses the degree (number) that best matches the observation and then sums and takes the average of all the comparisons made, for example, as in five-point scales.

task orientation The teacher's use of practices that help maintain an instructional focus by managing classroom activities efficiently, handling misbehavior with a minimum disruption to the class and reducing instructional time devoted to clerical duties to provide students the maximum opportunity to learn.

thematic notes A form of narrative reporting in which facts are recorded in traditional outline form, according to predesignated categories of observation, much like a detective at the scene of a crime who jots down facts about suspects, motives, times and places.

visual maps A form of reporting in which pictures portray the spatial relationships among physical objects in a classroom, such as learning centers, reference libraries, groups at work.

REFERENCES

Borich, G. (2004). *Effective teaching methods,* (5th ed.). Upper Saddle River, NJ: Prentice-Hall/Merrill.

Borich, G. (2003). *Observation Skills for Effective Teaching,* (4th ed.), Upper Saddle River, NJ: Prentice-Hall/Merrill.

Borich, G. and Tombari, M. (2004). *Educational assessment for the elementary and middle school classroom,* (2nd ed.). Upper Saddle River, NJ: Prentice-Hall/Merrill.

Borich, G., & Tombari, M. (1997). *Educational psychology: A contemporary approach, 2nd edition.* New York: Addison-Wesley Longman.

Canning, C. (1991). What teachers say about reflection. *Educational Leadership, 48*(6), 69–87.

Cantrell, S. C. (1998/1999). Effective teaching and literacy learning: A look inside primary classrooms. *The Reading Teacher, 52*(4), 370–378.

Compton-Lilly, C. (2000). "Staying on Children": Challenging stereotypes about urban parents. *Language Arts, 77*(5), 420–427.

Emmer, E., Evertson, C., & Worsham, M. (2003). *Classroom management for secondary teachers* (3rd ed.). Englewood Cliffs, NJ: Prentice-Hall.

Interstate New Teacher Assessment and Support Consortium (INTASC) (1992). *Model standards for beginning teacher licensing and development: A resource for state dialogue.* Retrieved July 30, 2003 from http://www.ccsso.org/intascst.html

Richardson, V. (1997). Constructivist teaching and teacher education: Theory and practice. In V. Richardson (Ed.), *Constructivist teacher education: Building new understandings* (pp. 3–14). Washington, DC: Falmer Press.

Sanford, A. J., & Garrod, S. C. (1981). *Understanding written language.* New York: John Wiley & Sons.

Sternberg, R. (1995). *The nature of insight.* Cambridge, MA: MIT Press.

Taylor, B. M., Pearson, P. D., Clark, K. F., & Walpole, S. (1999). Effective schools/accomplished teachers. *The Reading Teacher, 53*(2), 156–159.

Walqui, A. (2000). Access and engagement: Program design and instructional approaches for immigrant students in secondary school [Monograph]. *Language in Education: Theory and Practice 94*(Topics in Immigrant Education 4). Washington, DC: Center for Applied Linguistics.